Holy Things, Holy Actions, Holy Places

7th Chapter

AuthorHouse™
1663 Liberty Drive
Bloomington, IN 47403
www.authorhouse.com
Phone: 1 (800) 839-8640

Published by AuthorHouse 02/05/2018

ISBN: 978-1-5462-6183-4 (sc)
ISBN: 978- 1-5462-6184-1 (e)

Library of Congress Control Number: 2018911476

Print information available on the last page.

This book is printed on acid-free paper.

authorHOUSE®

SACRAMENTALS

ACKNOWLEDGEMENTS

We are grateful to many people for the completion of this work:

The Parish priest of St Benedict Church,
Father Vincent Arulanandam, for his encouragement, support and assistance;
Vicar General, Monsignor Michel Francis for permission to use photographs from the Archdiocese;
Parish Priest of the Parish of the Most Pure Heart of Mary,
Fr. Cleophas Joseph for assistance from his parish;
Monsignor Patrick Anthony and the Nuns of the Benedictine Abbey of Our Lady of the Assumption for their support and assistance.

Loyola Devaux our ever willing editor for her meticulous work.

Glenn Wilson for the design of the front and back covers;
Berthia Nickson for photographs from the Parish of the most Pure Heart of Mary;
Estellita Louisy for photography *The sign of the cross;*
Kevon George of Diamond Studios for photography of church buildings and liturgical vessels;
Patrick Dujon for Artwork *The washing of the feet.*

Parishioners of St Benedict Church and the Basilica of the Immaculate Conception and The Most Pure heart of Mary for use of their photographs.
Our families, for their patience and support.

FOREWORD

Greetings to all. With gratitude to God, as the parish priest of St. Benedict parish, I am privileged to appreciate the hard work of the members of 7th Chapter, of St. Benedict, Morne Fortune parish in bringing out this edifying book on SACRAMENTALS. These members are very strong in their faith and devotional practices. Their lives have become edifying and witnessing as they feel the moral responsibility of infusing the same faith in others, especially in the hearts and minds of the youth and the children. These women are very well learned persons who have worked in the schools and universities at various levels. I greatly acknowledge their dedication and commitment in attempting to teach Catholic children about Catholic faith through their way of life and especially their writings.

SACRAMENTALS are Holy things, Holy actions, Holy places *of which the church makes use to obtain for us from God, through her intercession, spiritual and temporal favors.* Sacramentals are channels of grace and can obtain for us these benefits: like Actual graces, Forgiveness of venial sins, Remission of temporal punishment, Health of body and material blessings and Protection from evil spirits. These are the means to our salvation.

Many faithful attend Holy Mass and various devotions in our churches and observe the use of the Sacramentals but don't know their names or purpose (Not only in our churches but even in our homes, health centers, schools, work places etc.). We probably have Sacramentals around us and do not even notice them. The book is therefore an attempt to teach and encourage Catholic Christians and any other interested persons in the following ways:

1. To get to know the names of these items used in the Catholic Liturgy and ceremonies;
2. To understand the religious significance of each item and the reason for its use, either in the liturgy or privately;
3. To assist in the faith formation of young and even older persons;
4. To encourage Catholics, young and old and those in between to pay more attention to and to appreciate our rich and beautiful Catholic religion, ceremonies and treasures.

The format is very simple and the language so easy for young and old to understand. Once again, I admire and appreciate the tremendous work of the members of the 7th chapter.

Sacramentals are easy tools for us to use to keep our focus on God and his saints. These items are given to us by God because He wants us to always come to Him with our requests and prayers. Use your sacramentals daily to strengthen your spiritual and prayer life and see where God will take you.

MAY GOD BLESS YOU ALL.
Fr. Vincent Sagayaraj Arulanandam MSFS
Parish Priest
Saint Benedict Parish
Morne Fortune, Castries.

SACRAMENTALS

Sacramentals are associated with Christian worship especially in the Roman Catholic Church. They help believers to feel and to think of things that are good. Therefore, they help them to put their minds on God and anything that is Holy. They are helpful but are not really necessary. There are many different Sacramentals. They come in the form of holy things, holy actions and holy places. They enable believers to focus on holy people, special holy events or special things and places associated with holiness.

To understand the purpose of Sacramentals we need to go back to the early establishment of the Church. At that time, most followers could not read or write. Therefore, church leaders found it necessary to present their teachings in a manner that would make ideas easy to understand. People needed to see and behave in a manner that would cause them to focus on things spiritual. For example, in the case of Jesus and His birth, people were presented with the crib. On seeing it, they would get a sense of the humility of Jesus. They would also understand the motherly care of Mary, His earthly Mother and the role of Joseph as father and protector. Most importantly, the crib or crèche as it is often called, stirs up a sense of family togetherness and love.

As noted earlier, the purpose of all Sacramentals is to put the mind of believers on holiness. That means to make us more aware of our faith, to make our devotions simple and to remind us that grace is available in the very simple actions and simple places of our daily lives. As long as we have a true disposition of faith that is we believe in the teachings of the Church, God's grace is available through all the Sacramentals of the Catholic Church.

HOLY THINGS

Altar

An altar is usually a table- like structure upon which offerings such as sacrifices are made for religious purposes. In the Catholic Church, at the consecration, the changing of the bread and wine into the Body and Blood of Jesus takes place on the altar during Holy Mass.

Altars could be natural objects or man-made. Some materials used in constructing altars are stone, earth, wood, metal, bricks and marble. At the Our Lady of Assumption Abbey, Mount of Prayer in Coubaril, Castries, an example of a stone altar can be seen.

In the Catholic Church a consecrated altar carries an altar stone beneath which a relic of a saint is embedded. An altar which has not been consecrated is known as an altar table and it does not contain a relic. A relic is a memorial of a saint, martyr, or other holy person, that has been preserved just as we preserve small items belonging to our ancestors. It may be an item of clothing, a body part or something associated with someone we hold in high regard.

The main altar in a Church must be so positioned to allow the entire congregation to visually follow any ceremony taking place there. Apart from the main altar there can be side altars if space permits. A side altar can be devoted to the honour of the Sacred Heart of Jesus and one to the Immaculate Heart of Mary. Every human heart has an invisible altar where the war between the flesh and the Spirit rages. When we surrender areas of our lives to the control of the Holy Spirit, we are laying that area on the altar before God.

The Bible makes reference to the use of altars in both the New and Old Testaments. Some of these include:

- "And Noah built an altar unto the Lord; and took of every clean beast, and of every clean fowl, and offered burnt offerings on the altar" *Genesis 8:20,*
- "If you are offering your gift at the altar and there remember that your brother has something against you, leave your gift there before the altar. First be reconciled to your brother, and then come and offer your gift". *Matthew 5: 23-24.*

Blessed Ashes

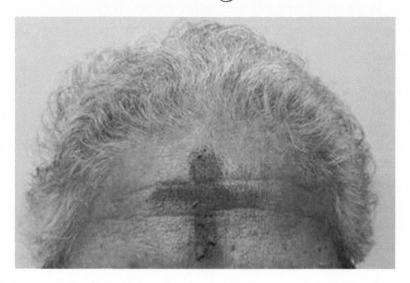

Blessed ashes are used in the Liturgy once only in the Church year – that is on Ash Wednesday – the first day of the Lenten Season, hence the name Ash Wednesday.

The ashes are obtained by burning blessed dried palm fronds of previous Palm Sundays. Unused blessed palms are burnt and the ashes reserved. These ashes are blessed by the priest on Ash Wednesday and used in the ceremony when the priest makes a sign of the cross on the foreheads of Catholics saying at the same time the words, "Remember man that you are dust and to dust you must return". This is to remind us that we are descended from Adam the first human being who was created by God, using soil from the earth and breathing life into him.

Throughout the Bible, ashes have been used as a form of penance. The Ninevites wore sack-cloth and sat in ashes as penance for their sins, after Jonah preached to them about repentance. *John 3: 5-6.*

Others used ashes on their heads as a sign of mourning and humiliation. *Ezekiel 27: 30-31.*

Blessed Oils

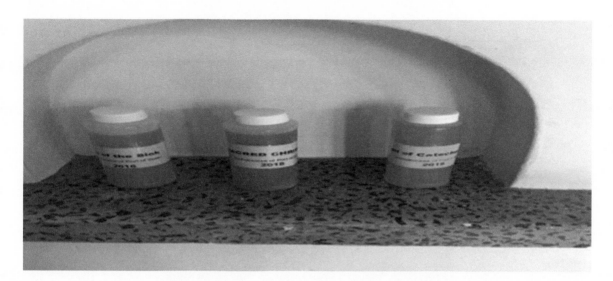

The use of oil is very important in the Church's Liturgy. Oil is used in the administering of the sacraments of Baptism, Confirmation, Holy Orders and also for anointing the sick and the dying.

Holy Oil is pure olive oil perfumed with balm and blessed by the Bishop during the Chrism Mass on the Wednesday of Holy Week.

There are three types of Holy Oils:

- Oil of the Catechumens used in the Baptismal Ceremony for anointing the candidate, before the water ceremony
- Oil of Chrism used in the ceremony of Confirmation and in the ceremony of Holy Orders when priests and bishops are consecrated
- Oil of the Sick used in anointing the sick and the dying

Oil of Catechumens and Chrism bestow the grace of the Holy Spirit.
Oil of the Sick bestows healing and graces on the sick and dying.
Blessed oils are also used in consecrating new cathedrals, churches and altars in churches *Exodus 29: 22-30.*

Blessed Salt

Throughout the ages salt has always been a precious commodity. Salt was used as wages for Roman soldiers; hence the word "salary" was derived from the word salt. Salt was and still is used as a preservative for meats and to savour food.

In ancient times salt became a symbol of incorruptibility. Salt – blessed salt can be used for safety – sprinkled in homes or across thresholds for safety. A few grains can be used in drinking water and in cooking.

In the earlier part of the 20th century, before Vatican II, a tiny bit of salt was put on the tongue of infants and others receiving the sacrament of Baptism. However, this is no longer a part of the baptism ceremony. In the New Testament, Jesus mentions that each of us is salt for the rest of mankind. "You are the salt of the earth," *Matthew 5:13*.

Blessed Cake
(Bonbon Benni)

In the Catholic Church it is a common practice to serve blessed cake to the congregation at the end of certain ceremonies. Some of these ceremonies are First Communion, First Communion anniversaries and other observances such as special feast days or at the end of an Ordination ceremony. It is a mark of togetherness and it is like a mini feast.

'Bonbon benni' is normally a simple cake, like a flat cake or sweet bread that is cut into small pieces. It is sometimes referred to as 'pen benni' or blessed bread. At the end of the service the celebrant raises his hand over the basket(s) and blesses the cake and bread. Then the ushers or people, who have been selected to do so, take the containers with the cake or bread to the doorway to make sure that everyone is served.

Candles

Candles are lit before an image of our Lord as well as before images of the saints. The lighted candle symbolizes a prayer offering where we present our petitions to the Lord and ask the saints to pray with us and to pray for us at the time of our direst needs. This light, as it is kept burning, also shows our desire to remain in God's presence as we go through our daily duties at home and in the workplace.

Candles lighted before Christ's image also show our reverence for Him who deserves our adoration and thanksgiving and who alone can forgive our sins and bring us back into a deeper relationship with Him.

Many Christians light candles as an aid to prayer. In Catholic Churches, the faithful place a lighted candle by a statue of Jesus, Mary or one of the saints. These are called votive candles. They are symbols of the prayers the worshiper is offering for himself or herself, or for other people. Catholics practice this not to honour the image itself but the one it truly represents.

Candles come in various colours, e.g. White, red, pink, and purple. They are used throughout the year on special occasions, such as baptisms and funerals. The Advent wreath, for example, uses all these colours. The white represents Christ.

The Pascal candle is a sacred symbol of Christ. The wax of the candle symbolizes Christ's sacred body while the flame and light show him to be the WORD of the Father enlightening everyone who comes into the world, "Your word is a lamp to my feet and a light to my path" *Psalm 119:105*. The Paschal candle is blessed and lit every year at Easter, and is used throughout the Paschal season which ends on the feast of the Ascension. Throughout the year the Paschal Candle is lit on special occasions, such as baptisms and funerals.

Crucifixes

A crucifix is a cross with the effigy of Jesus on it. It is a depiction of the lifeless body of Jesus while a cross, on the other hand, is a vertical beam with a horizontal cross bar. There is no image of the body of Christ on it.

A crucifix can be found on the Rosary of the Blessed Virgin and on many items in Catholic homes. Catholics commonly display a crucifix rather than a cross as the crucifixion story is very important for our salvation. At the time of Jesus, death by crucifixion was considered the most shameful and most painful way to die.

Look at the crucifix again! Very, very big nails were driven into each palm, then the feet were crossed over and a nail was driven from the top to the sole of the feet.

A crucifix is usually positioned in a Catholic Church so that it is immediately visible as one enters the church. It is to remind us of the type of death that Jesus Christ suffered for our sins. According to Pope Benedict XV1, "the Crucifix is the supremely distinctive sign of him who announces the Gospel: a sign of love and peace, a call to conversion and reconciliation". *Pope Quotes 2018.*

In addition, the Catholic writer Ann Ball writes, "The church pays such honour to the crucifix that sacraments are administered, Mass is celebrated and all acts of worship are performed in the presence of a crucifix" *Ball 1991:81.*

Holy Water

Water, as we know, is used for cleaning and the use of water traditionally symbolizes a cleansing process. When Naaman, the leper, went to Elisha for healing, Elisha sent him to wash seven times in the river Jordon *2 Kings 5:1-19*.

In the Catholic Church, holy water is water that has been blessed by a priest or any member of the clergy for the baptismal ceremony, the blessing of persons, places and objects. In the New Testament, John refers to the profound transforming power of water in Baptism, "Unless a man is born of water and the Holy Spirit, he cannot enter into the Kingdom of God" *John 3:5*.

Holy water is normally available at the entrance of Catholic churches so that the faithful may bless themselves as they enter. There are many ways to use Holy Water. Some of them are as follows:

1. Bless yourself – You can never have too much grace or blessings in your life.

2. Bless your house – You can sprinkle holy water in your home yourself, or have a priest formally bless your home using holy water as part of the blessing ceremony.
3. Bless your car – You can also have a priest bless your car with holy water
4. Bless people - the sick, your family, children, your work place etc.

The author Ball, gives some idea of the prayers said by the priest in the blessing of water:

- "May that creature of yours, water, serve to cast out demons and to banish disease. May everything the water sprinkles in the homes and gathering of the faithful be delivered from all that is unclean and hurtful. By the sprinkling of this water, may all that is opposed to safety and peace of the occupants of these homes be banished, so that in calling your Holy Name they may know the well-being they desire and be protected from every peril, through Jesus Christ" *Ball 1991:56*

Incense

The word "incense" is derived from the Latin *incendere* which means "to burn". Incense is also referred to as Holy Smoke. As we read in the Old Testament, God commanded His people to burn incense: "On this altar Aaron must burn fragrant incense each morning when he prepares the lamps, and in the evening twilight when Aaron puts the lamps back, he must burn it again. You must make these offerings of incense before Yahweh unfailingly from generation to generation" *Exodus 30:7-8.*

Incense is a sacramental used to venerate, bless, and sanctify. Its smoke conveys a sense of mystery and awe. It is a reminder of the sweet-smelling presence of our Lord. Its use adds a feeling of solemnity to the Mass. In addition, incense is used in various solemn processions, graveside services, the blessing and the dedication of new churches, cemeteries, and items such as new altars, new church bells, new sacred vessels and newly acquired copies of the Book of Gospels.

Incensing also suggests a "burnt offering" to God at which time one offers prayers of adoration, contrition, thanksgiving and supplication. Incense smoke symbolically purifies all that it touches and the rising smoke helps one to imagine prayers rising up to God, in the same way that the smoke rises up.

The priest puts incense into a vessel called the thurible, blesses it with the sign of the Cross without saying anything and then the deacon or altar servers swing the thurible so we can see the rising of the Holy Smoke. At the Easter Vigil, five grains of encapsulated incense (most often made to look like red nails) are embedded in the paschal candle. These five grains of incense represent the five wounds of Jesus Christ — one in each hand, one in each foot, and one made by the spear thrust into His side.

Liturgical Vessels

In the Catholic Church, liturgical vessels which are the sacred utensils used in the celebration of Mass and other liturgical events are very important.

The following liturgical vessels are the most commonly used:

Chalice:
The chalice is the Cup that contains the wine for consecration.

Ciborium:
The Ciborium is the container which holds the host. Unlike the chalice, the ciborium has a cover.

Cruets:

These are small containers which hold the water and wine to be used during Mass.

Intinction Set:

This is a vessel designed with two compartments to serve communion under both species.

Monstrance:

An ornate receptacle for exposing the Blessed Sacrament.

Tabernacle:

This is the place in the church where the consecrated hosts are kept. It can normally be identified by the single red light situated somewhere near it. This is the resting place of Jesus.

Pyx:

The pyx is a small round container used to carry the consecrated host.

Thurible:
The thurible is a metal censer for burning incense.

Liturgical Vestments

The garments which the priest wears when performing his sacred duties are referred to as vestments. Vestments are sacramentals because the church has designed them to inspire us and to help us to understand that the events at which they are worn are solemn and serious.

In the picture the priests are wearing a vestment referred to as Chausubles. This vestment (singular chausuble) is used at Mass and other church celebrations. The colour is purple because this picture was taken during Lent and Purple is the liturgical colour of that season.

The colours of a Catholic priest's vestments help the laity to know what feasts or occasions are being celebrated.

- Green is the colour of vestments used during Ordinary Time. (Ordinary Time is the rest of the year that is not the Christmas or Easter season — it's still important, it just has an unexciting name.)
- Purple or violet is used during Advent and Lent, and along with white and black, these colors may also be used at Funeral Masses.
- White and gold are most appropriate for Christmas and Easter.

- Red is used on feasts of the Passion of Jesus and for the Holy Spirit. Red is also worn for the feasts of martyred saints.
- Rose is used on the Third Sunday of Advent and the Fourth Sunday of Lent. The colour rose is worn as a sign of anticipated joy.

Church decorations and flowers may sometimes correspond with the vestment colours.

ALB

The Alb is a long white ankle length garment with long sleeves. The cord around the middle is called the cincture. In this picture it is green but is usually white or cream.

The cincture is a rope-like or ribbon-like article wrapped around or above the waist.

HUMERAL VEIL

The humeral veil is a vestment worn over the shoulders and covering the hands of the priest when he is holding a sacred vessel.

The priest uses this vestment at Benediction when he holds the Monstrance for the blessing of the people and also when he carries the Blessed Sacrament in procession.

STOLE

The STOLE is a long narrow rectangular vestment, which the priest wears around his neck with the ends hanging down.

It is used at Mass and also in nearly every other religious function, for example, funerals, the blessing of homes and other special occasions.

The deacon's stole varies a little because it is worn over the shoulder along the side.

Medals

Medals are Sacramentals used by Catholics. They are made from metal, plastic, stone or other material. These pieces are stamped, or engraved with pictures of what the medal is meant to represent. Then the medal is put on a chain or cord or brooch and hung around the neck or pinned to the dress. Catholics who wear medals do so to remind them to pray for grace and blessing in order to live a holy life. Usually a medal is a reminder of a Saint who has a special life story. For example, St. Anthony is named the finder of lost things, St Christopher, the Saint of travellers. The miraculous medal is universally worn and there are many stories associated with wearers of this symbol of confidence in the intercession of the Mother of God.

You should look up the story of Catherine Laboure' of France which tells the story of the miraculous medal.

Rosaries

The Rosary is a Scripture-based prayer. It begins with the Apostle's Creed which summarizes the great mysteries of the Catholic faith. The Lord's Prayer, which introduces each mystery, is from the Gospels: *Matthew 6 :5-14.*The first part of the Hail Mary is a combination of the angel's words announcing Christ's birth and Elizabeth's greeting to Mary. St Pius V officially added the second part of the Hail Mary.

The purpose of the rosary is to help keep in memory certain principal events or mysteries in the history of our salvation and to thank and praise God for them. All the mysteries of the rosary centre on significant events in the life of Christ.

When we pray the rosary, we are provided with the opportunity to meditate on the events in Jesus's life. The rosary is more than just repeating the words of Gabriel, "Hail Full of Grace, the Lord is with Thee" and Elizabeth "Blessed art thou among women, and blessed is the fruit of thy womb Jesus" from scripture. It is also about meditating on the twenty "mysteries". What are these mysteries?

As suggested by Pope St. John Paul II, the Joyful mysteries are said on Monday and Saturday, the Sorrowful on Tuesday and Friday, the Glorious on Wednesday and Sunday and the Luminous on Thursday.

The Mysteries of the Rosary are as follows:

The Joyful Mysteries
1. **The Annunciation** Mary learns that she has been chosen to be the mother of Jesus.
2. **The Visitation** Mary visits her cousin Elizabeth, who tells her that she will always be favoured among women.
3. **The Nativity** Jesus is born in a stable in Bethlehem.
4. **The Presentation** Mary and Joseph take the infant Jesus to the Temple to present Him to God.
5. **The Finding of Jesus in the Temple** Jesus is found in the Temple discussing His faith with the teachers.

The Sorrowful Mysteries
1. **The Agony in the Garden** Jesus prays in the Garden of Gethsemane on the night before He dies.
2. **The Scourging at the Pillar** Jesus is lashed with whips.
3. **The Crowning With Thorns** Jesus is mocked and crowned with thorns.
4. **The Carrying of the Cross** Jesus carries the cross that will be used to crucify him.
5. **The Crucifixion** Jesus is nailed to the cross and dies.

The Glorious Mysteries
1. **The Resurrection** God the Father raises Jesus from the dead.
2. **The Ascension** Jesus returns to His Father in heaven.
3. **The Coming of the Holy Spirit** The Holy Spirit comes to bring new life to the disciples.
4. **The Assumption of Mary** At the end of her life on earth, Mary is taken body and soul into heaven.
5. **The Coronation of Mary** Mary is crowned as Queen of Heaven and Earth.

The Mysteries of Light or the Luminous Mysteries
1. **The Baptism of Jesus in the River Jordan** God proclaims that Jesus is His beloved Son.
2. **The Wedding Feast at Cana** At Mary's request, Jesus performs His first miracle.
3. **The Proclamation of the Kingdom of God** Jesus calls all to conversion and service to the Kingdom.
4. **The Transfiguration of Jesus** Jesus is revealed in glory to Peter, James, and John.
5. **The Institution of the Eucharist** Jesus offers his Body and Blood at the Last Supper

Scapulars

A Scapular is a symbol to mark a person as belonging to a church group or confraternity. It is designed as a slender cord suspended over the shoulder to which is attached a small rectangular cloth resting on the chest and another resting on the back. The rectangular pieces of cloth depict sacred images which indicate the person to which the group's devotion is pledged.

The scapular was first used by the monks of the Benedictine order. These monks had as their rule, 'Ora et Labora' Latin for 'Work and Pray'. They offered all their work as a prayer to God. The monks who worked as field labourers, wore a brown apron to cover their whole dress or habit to protect it from becoming soiled. The laity of the parish who joined the monks at a later stage was also identified by wearing a scapular of the same colour but of a different style. In the traditional customs of the Church, symbols such as these are intended to remind us to commemorate life in the spiritual realm and to help us to live close to Jesus.

Some popular scapulars are, the Brown Scapulars of the Carmelite confraternity, the Blue scapular of Our Lady of the Immaculate Conception and the Red scapular of the Sacred Heart of Jesus.

Statues

A statue is a figure of a person which is made out of material such as clay, metal, wood or stone. Catholics do not worship idols, but have a long tradition of using statues in our churches because thousands of years ago, the average person could not read and understand the stories in the bible for themselves. Priests and scribes were the only people who were educated enough to read and understand the bible. The church therefore used statues, paintings and stained glass windows to visually portray the stories in the bible to show what people from that time period may have looked like.

Today we have photographs of grandparents to remember them by and share stories about who they were. In a nation's capital, certain buildings have statues of the president, war heroes or other public figures in order to honour them and preserve their memory. Here in St Lucia, in Constitution Park, the statue of the late Prime Minister, Sir John Compton, serves to remind us of his role in the development of St. Lucia.

In the Catholic Church there are statues of Jesus, Mary and the saints to honour and preserve their memory just as we do with important persons and loved ones, but we do not worship them. Statutes are Sacramentals that serve to help us in the development of our spiritual lives.

As Catholics, we want the lives of Jesus, of Mary and of the saints to be forever in our hearts and in our daily lives.

HOLY ACTIONS

Blessings

A Blessing is a Sacramental because it is a holy action. The persons giving the blessing normally either stretch their hand over the person or persons receiving it or they place their hand on the head or on any other part of the person being blessed. The very word blessing is beautiful. It makes you feel that the person using it has pleasant feelings towards you. We hear the word being used almost every day. Blessings have been given throughout the ages and there are many instances of it in the Old as well as in the New Testament.

In the Old Testament, especially in the book of Numbers, there are many references to 'blessings'. The word is repeated frequently in Chapter 6. There we read the following blessing which is very popular. It reads: "The Lord bless you and keep you, the Lord make His face to shine upon you, and be gracious unto you, and give you peace" *Numbers 6:22-24*.

When someone gives you a blessing you feel that they wish you peace and protection from harm or anything unpleasant that could make you uncomfortable. In the Bible there are several places where, instead of the word 'blessing', words like peace, love and protection are used. In each case, the reference means the same. It is to wish you well. Here are a few examples:

"The grace of the Lord Jesus Christ, and the love of God, and the fellowship of the Holy Spirit be with you all" *2nd Corinthians 13:14*.

In *Isaiah 43: 1-3*, we read about the constant love and protection of God.

Whenever someone blesses you even by saying something as simple as "God bless you", be sure to show your appreciation by saying, "Thank you." You, in turn, should adopt the practice of saying to others, "God bless you." You know it is a sure way of making others happy.

Bowing The Head

People bow when they want to show respect to someone whom they consider to be of higher authority. When it comes to matters related to God, we bow to show respect. That is why we bow our heads when prayers are being said. Priests, altar servers and worshipers bow before the crucifix and we often bow before the altar. The practice of bowing is very ancient.

There are several references to the practice in the bible.

In the Old Testament we have the following:

- "Then the man bowed low and worshipped the Lord". *Genesis 24:26.*
- "Then David said to the assembly, 'Now bless the Lord your God' and all the Assembly blessed the Lord, the God of their fathers and bowed low and did homage to the Lord and to the King" I *Chronicles 29:20.*

Paul says in the New Testament, "At the name of Jesus, every knee should bend in heaven and on earth". *Philippians 2:10.*

When we consider the significance of the act of bowing the head, we should do so readily at the appropriate times and we should never allow the thought of what others might think to deter us from doing so.

Genuflection

Genuflection is the act of bending either on one or both knees facing the altar. Roman Catholics genuflect as a mark of respect before they enter the pews and sit down in the church. They also do so when they leave the church. As they genuflect, they may say a silent prayer. When the Blessed Sacrament is exposed, they genuflect on both knees to show special reverence for the presence of Our Lord in the Blessed Sacrament. At that same time also, they may say a silent prayer such as, "My God, I adore you".

The practice of kneeling in genuflection is expressed in *Psalm 95: 6* in the words, "Come let us bow down, let us kneel before the Lord our Maker".

It appears that the act of kneeling to show respect is not only accepted by the Lord but it is expected because in *Romans 14: 11*, Paul reminds us, "It is written, as surely as I am the living God, everyone will kneel before Me and everyone will confess that I am God".

The Sign Of The Cross

In the name of the Father,   and of the Son,   and of the Holy,   Spirit.   Amen.

The sign of the cross not only causes us to think of God but it also demonstrates to anyone who observes that we are members of a group that believes in God. The sign of the cross is normally made with the right hand. We place the hand on the forehead as we say, "In the name of the Father", then we go down to the heart or chest as we say, "and of the Son", and then move to the left shoulder to say "Holy" and we end on the right shoulder with the word "Spirit" and end with "Amen".

As we can see, the sign of the cross puts in mind the Trinity, or the three persons in God as well as the fact that Jesus, the Son of God, died on the cross to save us. *Romans 5: 8 -11*

In fact, in Paul's letter to the Romans much of what he says, especially in Chapter 8, is devoted to the Spirit of God dwelling in three persons.

When we enter a Catholic church, we sign ourselves. At the same time, we should genuflect reverently to show respect for the Blessed Sacrament.

The sign of the cross is also a mark of respect for Jesus in the Holy Tabernacle. We use it as a quick sign of our gratitude for something, as a quick prayer whenever we face something important or challenging such as an examination, and sometimes when we are afraid. We should always be willing and proud to use it and it is a good Catholic practice to make the sign of the cross when walking past a Catholic Church.

Washing Of The Feet

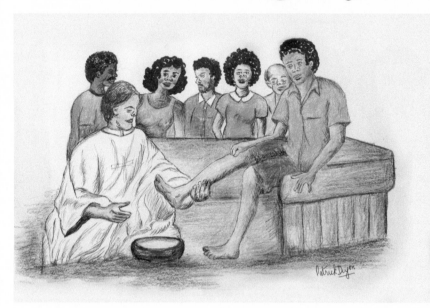

The washing of the feet is a religious rite which began on Holy Thursday at Jesus' last supper with his apostles. Before he sat down to eat, Jesus poured water into a basin, wrapped a towel around Him and washed the feet of the apostles and dried them with the towel. The apostles were somewhat uneasy to have Jesus wash their feet and Peter, one of the twelve, tried to object but Jesus told him it had to be done.

After the meal, Jesus said to the apostles, "Do you understand what I have done to you? You call Me Master and Lord and you are right, for so I am. If I then, your Lord and Master have washed your feet, you also must wash one another's feet. I have given you an example that as I have done, you also may do." *John 13:12-15*

The washing of the feet by Jesus was an important lesson in humility and service to others. This ceremony continues today by Catholics at the mass celebrated on the evening of Holy Thursday. Twelve men, representing the twelve apostles, are chosen to have their feet washed by the celebrant during the Mass. Sometimes women are invited to be part of the twelve and to have their feet washed.

HOLY PLACES

From ancient times Christians have a tradition of visiting holy places on a regular basis. In the time of Jesus, the Jews made pilgrimages every year to the Temple in Jerusalem. The Temple was considered a holy place. Luke tells the story of Joseph and Mary making the journey with the child Jesus when he was twelve years old. *Luke 2: 41-42.*

After the death of Jesus, the early Christians journeyed to the places where significant events in His life had taken place. The place of His birth in Bethlehem, the site of His crucifixion and His burial site are some examples. They were considered holy places and having the privilege of making a pilgrimage to these places was considered a tremendous source of grace.

Over time the church added sites of apparitions such as Fatima and Lourdes, places where Saints or Holy persons lived and died, beautiful places dedicated to worship. These exist in the locations of the early church sites, in places such as Jerusalem, Rome and other countries in Europe. Christians from all over the world make pilgrimages to these places annually. For Catholics, such a visit is a Sacramental - another source of tremendous grace.

However, the church has taught that we do not have to travel to far off places to make a pilgrimage. We can visit holy places in our Parishes or in other parts of the country. In St Lucia, we have several holy places that Catholics can visit or to which they can make pilgrimages.

Some of these are:

The Basilica of the Immaculate Conception in Castries

The Abbey of Our Lady of the Assumption at Coubaril, Morne Fortune

The Shrine of St. Lucy in Micoud

The Chapel of our Lady of Lourdes at Bois D'Orange

As well as all the parish churches in St Lucia.

Martha Isaac is a retired university lecturer. She is the author of the devotional 'Reclaiming our Citadel: Reflections on Widowhood'. She belongs to the Parish of St Benedict and recently retired from her work as catechist in that parish. She is actively involved in the work of the Carmelite Tertiary Chapter of St. Teresa of Avila. She has two grown daughters and four grandchildren.

Emma Bernard-Joseph is a retired Administrative Professional Secretary and Refractionist. She was last employed as the Manager of Eye Care Saint Lucia, a subsidiary of Saint Lucia Blind Welfare Association, a non-profit organisation working with and for blind and visually impaired persons. She is an active member of the St. Benedict Parish, being very involved in all matters of Parish life.

Martha Celestin is a retired Administrative Professional Secretary and a devout member of St Benedict Parish Confraternities. Martha Celestin started her working life as a teacher at a Catholic School. There she taught religious instruction and she also prepared children for receiving their First Holy Communion. She subsequently changed her career to the secretarial field embarking on a career as an Administrative Professional Secretary.

Julia Hennecart is a retired educator having served as principal of a Catholic Girls' school for a number of years. She is a devout member of St Benedict Parish Confraternities. On her retirement, she became very active in parish life. She served as catechist preparing children for the Sacrament of Confirmation. She has also served as a minister of the Eucharist.
She is mother of five and grandmother of ten.

Ingrid Millar has given thirty years of service to the Saint Lucia Tourist Board. She worked with at least seven Directors of Tourism as Executive Secretary and now serves as Administrative Manager. She is actively involved in the work of St Benedict Parish. Ingrid enjoys photography and family moments with her husband and two sons.

Agatha Mortley-Modeste is a retired educator whose career spanned forty years involved teaching at various levels of the education system and serving as an administrator. She is a devout Roman Catholic with experience as an instructor in the doctrine which started from her secondary school when, as a member of the Legion of Mary, her duty was to prepare children for receiving their First Holy Communion. This educator regards gaining full knowledge of her faith as a life-long journey and she is very keen on sharing such knowledge especially with the youth. Agatha has two grown children.

Esther Stephen is a retired Elementary School Principal. She taught all classes from kindergarten to Grade eight and beyond. She is a devout member of St Benedict confraternities. She comes from a family of fourteen. Her own family consists of five children with the four remaining adults holding their own successfully in the communities where they currently reside. She continues to be passionate about cooking, gardening and family.

EDITOR- Loyola Devaux has retired after teaching for over forty years. The last last twenty years were spent as a lecturer at the Sir Arthur Lewis Community College in Communication Studies. She has led an active life as Head of department for over a decade, as well as being involved in various areas of her church community and social work on a voluntary basis. She is married, has five grown children and nine grandchildren.

REFERENCES

Ball, Ann. 1991. *A Handbook of Catholic Sacramentals*. Our Sunday Visitor Publishing Division: Huntington, Indiana.

Hahn, Scott. 2000. *Signs of Life, 40 Catholic Customs and their Biblical Roots*. Doubleday: New York

Lambing, Andrew Arnold. *1892 The Sacramentals Of The Holy Catholic Church*. Benziger Brothers: New York, Cincinnati, Chicago.